THE UNIVERSE
THE SOLAR SYSTEM

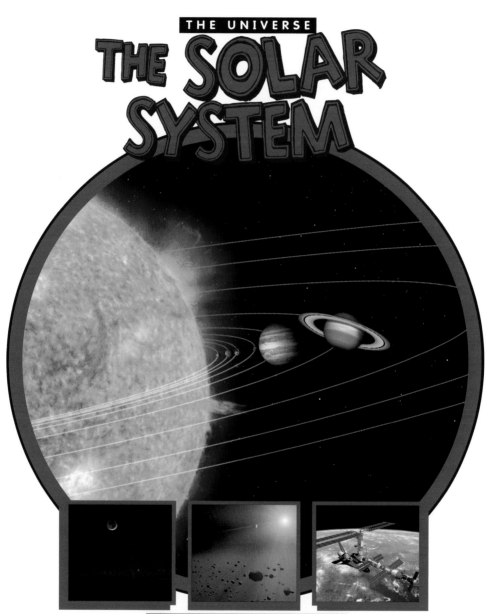

ABDO
Publishing Company

A Buddy Book by Fran Howard

VISIT US AT

www.abdopublishing.com

Published by ABDO Publishing Company, 8000 West 78th Street, Edina, Minnesota 55439.

Printed in the United States.

Editor: Sarah Tieck
Contributing Editor: Michael P. Goecke
Graphic Design: Maria Hosley
Cover Image: Photos.com
Interior Images: Will Crocker (page 5); Lushpix (page 17, 30); NASA: JPL-Caltech (page 11), Jet Propulsion Laboratory (page 13, 15, 19, 28, 29), JPL / Space Science Institute (page 15), Marshall Space Flight Center (page 27); Photos.com (page 23, 25, 28); Stocktrek Images (page 7).

Library of Congress Cataloging-in-Publication Data

Howard, Fran, 1953-
  The solar system / Fran Howard.
      p. cm. — (The universe)
  Includes index.
  ISBN 978-1-59928-930-4
  1. Solar system—Juvenile literature. I. Title.

  QB501.3.H69 2008
  523.2--dc22
                                        2007027792

Table Of Contents

Our Solar System

When people look up into the night sky, they can often see the moon. Sometimes, they can even see planets glowing brightly. These are just a few parts of our solar system.

Our solar system is very big. It includes our sun and everything that orbits it. There are planets, moons, comets, asteroids, and other space objects moving around our sun.

Some scientists think our solar system
is more than 4 billion years old!

The Milky Way

In space, groups of stars form **galaxies**. Galaxies also contain dust, gas, and other space objects.

Our galaxy is called the Milky Way. The Milky Way is filled with stars and solar systems.

Our solar system is part of the Milky Way. And, our sun is one of the many stars in this galaxy.

Some scientists think the Milky Way could have 400 billion stars!

A Closer Look

Each solar system contains a star orbited by many space objects, such as planets. The star is the center of the solar system. Planets and other space objects circle the star because of gravity's pull.

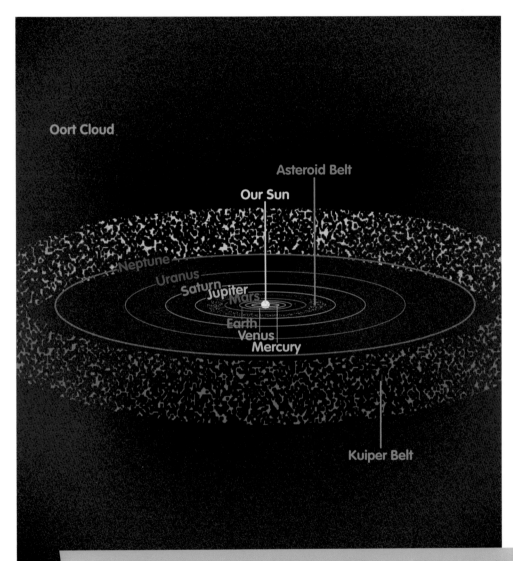

Oort Cloud

Asteroid Belt

Our Sun

Neptune
Uranus
Saturn
Jupiter
Mars
Earth
Venus
Mercury

Kuiper Belt

In our solar system, eight planets orbit the sun. There are also dwarf planets, comets, asteroids, meteoroids, and moons.

It is possible to see many stars from Earth. But, our sun is the only star in our solar system. It is our solar system's center.

The word *solar* means "sun." Without the sun, there wouldn't be a solar system or life on Earth!

The sun provides light and heat to the entire solar system. This affects each part of it in different ways. The sun makes some space objects very hot, while others stay very cold.

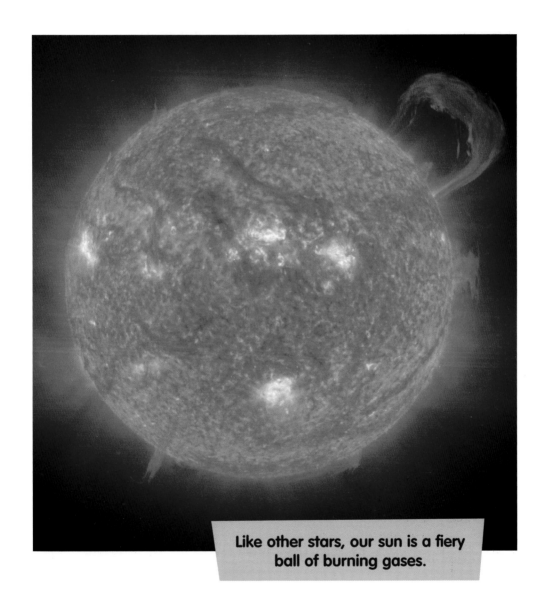

Like other stars, our sun is a fiery
ball of burning gases.

Circling The Sun

Eight planets orbit the sun. The planets closest to the sun are Mercury, Venus, Earth, and Mars. These planets have hard, rocky surfaces.

The planets farthest from the sun are Jupiter, Saturn, Uranus, and Neptune. These planets are known as gas giants. They are made of gases, liquids, and ice. They do not have a solid surface.

The Sun

There are three known dwarf planets that orbit our sun. They are named Ceres, Pluto, and Eris.

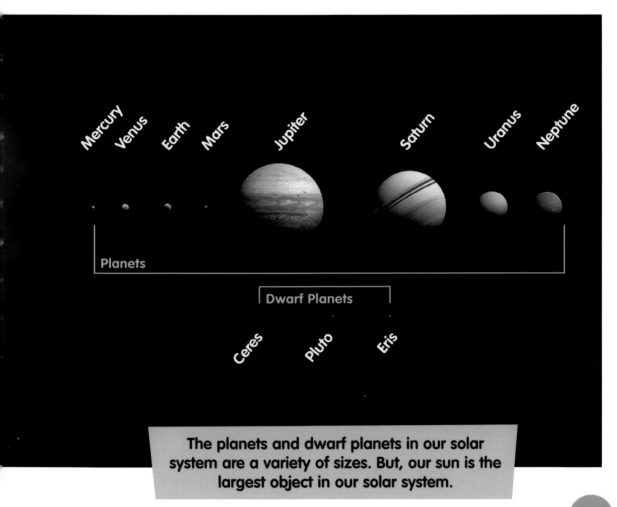

The planets and dwarf planets in our solar system are a variety of sizes. But, our sun is the largest object in our solar system.

Floating In Space

Many moons orbit the planets. Earth has only one moon. But, scientists have discovered more than 100 moons in our solar system!

Altogether, the gas giants have 162 moons. Jupiter has the most with 63. Saturn has 59 moons, Uranus has 27, and Neptune has 13.

Rhea is one of Saturn's moons.

Triton is Neptune's largest moon.

Deimos *(left)* and Phobos *(right)* are Mars's moons.

Ganymede is one of Jupiter's moons.

Moons can be similar to planets. Some have volcanoes, mountains, and oceans.

Asteroids are space rocks. They come in many sizes and are found throughout our solar system. Some areas of the solar system have millions of them!

Comets are also found in our solar system. They are round and icy, like giant snowballs in space.

Beyond Neptune, there is a part of the solar system called the Kuiper belt. This area is filled with large ice and rock objects. These include the dwarf planets Pluto and Eris.

The asteroid belt is full of large space rocks. It is located between Mars and Jupiter.

17

Far, Far Away

Our solar system is very large. It would take many years to see all of it! This is why scientists do not know much about some areas. Some space objects are so far away that no **spacecraft** from Earth has ever visited!

The *New Horizons* spacecraft was launched in 2006. It is expected to fly by the dwarf planet Pluto around 2015.

Some scientists say the heliopause is the boundary of our solar system. It is where our solar system meets outer space. Scientists still have much to learn about these faraway parts of the solar system.

Heliopause

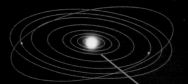

Sun and Planets

The sun is the source of solar wind. Solar wind is created when the sun's energy escapes into space. It pushes all the dust and gas toward the heliopause.

Discovering Our Solar System

For a long time, people believed Earth was the center of the universe. They didn't know the sun was the center of our solar system.

In the 1500s, Polish astronomer Nicolaus Copernicus said the planets circle the sun. This was a very important discovery. Many people said this idea was wrong. But eventually, it was proven correct.

Italian scientist Galileo Galilei was famous for his ideas. He agreed with Copernicus about the solar system. But, many other people said their ideas were wrong.

Exploring Our Solar System

In 1957, the Russians **launched** *Sputnik 1* into space. This was the first **spacecraft** to orbit Earth.

Since then, there have been many **missions**. Spacecraft from Earth have flown near all eight planets. Some spacecraft have even landed on Venus, Mars, and Earth's moon!

American astronaut Neil Armstrong walked on the moon
on July 21, 1969. He arrived on the *Apollo 11* spacecraft.
He is the first human to walk on a space object.

Astronauts learn about our solar system by traveling into space. Some have even lived in **space stations**!

The first U.S. space station was *Skylab*. It orbited from 1973 to 1979. Then, astronauts lived in *Mir* from 1989 to 1999. People from 12 countries visited this Russian space station.

Since 2000, astronauts have been working to build the *International Space Station*. It replaced *Mir*, which fell back to Earth in 2001.

Astronauts on space stations conduct many experiments.
Their findings help people learn more about our solar system.

Fact Trek

The dwarf planet Ceres is the largest known asteroid in the asteroid belt!

The *Dawn* spacecraft is expected to explore Ceres around 2015.

In our solar system, Earth is the only planet known to have life on it.

People and animals are among the living things that flourish on Earth.

For many years, scientists said Pluto was the ninth planet. Now, it is considered a dwarf planet. Many scientists are still discussing this.

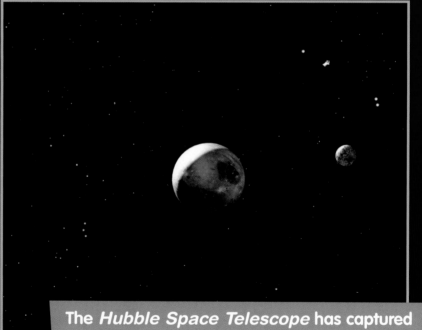

The *Hubble Space Telescope* has captured images of Pluto and its moons. These images help scientists learn new facts.

Voyage To Tomorrow

Scientists make new discoveries about our solar system every day. They are always working to learn more.

The United States plans to continue exploring the solar system. It expects to complete the *International **Space Station*** by 2010.

The U.S. space program hopes to send astronauts back to Earth's moon by 2020. And later, astronauts may travel to Mars.

Spacecraft have landed on Mars. But, no humans have visited it.

Important Words

galaxy a large group of stars and planets.

launch to send off with force.

mission the sending of spacecraft to perform specific jobs.

space station an orbiting space laboratory where people live and study space.

spacecraft a vehicle that travels in space.

Web Sites

To learn more about the **solar system**, visit ABDO Publishing Company on the World Wide Web. Web sites about the **solar system** are featured on our Book Links page. These links are routinely monitored and updated to provide the most current information available.

www.abdopublishing.com

INDEX